Science Matters
VOLCANOES

Jennifer Nault

WEIGL PUBLISHERS INC.

Published by Weigl Publishers Inc.
350 5th Avenue, Suite 3304, PMB 6G
New York, NY USA 10118-0069
Web site: www.weigl.com
Copyright 2005 WEIGL PUBLISHERS INC.

Library of Congress Cataloging-in-Publication Data

Nault, Jennifer.
  Volcanoes / Jennifer Nault.
       p. cm. -- (Science matters)
  Includes index.
  ISBN 978-1-59036-211-2 (lib. bdg. : alk. paper) ISBN 978-1-59036-253-2 (softcover)
  1. Volcanoes--Juvenile literature. I. Title. II. Series.
  QE521.3.N385 2005
  551.21--dc22

                                  2004004137

Printed in the United States of America
2 3 4 5 6 7 8 9 0 08

Project Coordinator Tina Schwartzenberger
Substantive Editor Heather Kissock **Copy Editor** Frances Purslow
Design Terry Paulhus **Layout** Bryan Pezzi
Photo Researcher Ellen Bryan

Photograph Credits

Every reasonable effort has been made to trace ownership and to obtain permission to reprint copyright material. The publishers would be pleased to have any errors or omissions brought to their attention so that they may be corrected in subsequent printings.

Cover: Volcano from Photos.com
CORBIS/MAGMA: pages 9 (Royalty Free), 19 (Roger Ressmeyer); **DAVID R. FRAZIER Photolibrary, Inc.:** pages 16, 18; **Bryan Pezzi:** pages 12-13; **Photos.com:** pages 3T, 3M, 3B, 17, 21, 22T, 22B, 23T, 23B; **United States Geological Survey:** pages 1 (Cascades Volcano Observatory/Richard P. Hoblitt), 4 (J.D. Griggs), 6, 7T (G.E. Ulrich), 7M (Alaska Division of Geological and Geophysical Surveys/C. Nye), 7B (J.D. Griggs), 8, 10 (J.D. Griggs), 11T (Cascades Volcano Observatory/ Austin Post), 11B (J.D. Griggs), 14T (Cascades Volcano Observatory/Harry Glicken), 14B (Cascades Volcano Observatory/Lyn Topinka).

Contents

Studying Volcanoes

An **erupting** volcano is a sight to see. When a volcano erupts, gases and dust fly into the sky. Falling ash and red-hot **lava** cover large areas. These materials can destroy everything they touch. An erupting volcano can put people who live nearby in great danger.

Volcanoes erupt because of powerful forces at work deep inside Earth. Scientists are not sure what causes these forces to occur. They study volcanoes to solve this mystery.

Kilauea is a volcano located on the southernmost island of Hawai'i. It is one of Earth's most active volcanoes.

Volcano Facts

Did you know that the circular, funnel-shaped opening at the top of a volcano is called a crater? Read on to learn more about volcanoes, lava, and volcanic eruptions.

- Materials spurting out of a volcano are very hot. They are about 2,000° Fahrenheit (1,093° Celsius). This is hot enough to cook a hot dog in one second!

- Lava can travel 120 miles (193 kilometers) per hour.

- Lava is **magma** that has come to Earth's surface. There are two kinds of lava. Fluid lava, called *pahoehoe*, flows quickly. Sticky lava, called *a'a*, moves more slowly.

- Earth's largest volcano is Mauna Loa. It rises 2.5 miles (4 km) above sea level. Mauna Loa covers about half of the island of Hawai'i.

- Volcanoes helped create Earth. They added new rock to the land and gases to the **atmosphere**.

- Some people choose to live near volcanoes. This is because the land is good for farming.

What is a Volcano?

A volcano is an opening in Earth's surface. Magma and gas rise through the opening and burst forth. The opening is usually found at the top of a cone-shaped mountain. These mountains are often called volcanoes, too.

Volcanoes are not all the same. They can look very different. Layers of magma form volcanoes. The size and shape of a volcano depend on the magma's thickness. The type and timing of eruptions also change how volcanoes look.

● Crater Peak is on Mount Spurr in Alaska. It began erupting at least 6,000 years ago.

Types of Volcanoes

Scientists group volcanoes into three main types. The types are cinder cones, composite volcanoes, and shield volcanoes.

Cinder cones are steep and cone-like in shape. They are formed from tiny, glassy pieces of volcanic rock. These pieces settle around the **vent**.

Composite volcanoes are also cone-shaped. They are larger than cinder cones because they have erupted many times from the same vent. Composite volcanoes are made from alternating layers of lava, volcanic ash, and cinders. Cinders are pieces of coal, wood, or other material that is still hot and glowing but no longer burning.

Shield volcanoes look like large mounds. They are formed by fluid lava made of **basalt**. This kind of lava flows quite far. It creates soft-sloped mountains.

Moving Earth

Earth's surface is made of a thin layer of rock called the crust. The crust is broken into twelve large pieces called tectonic plates. A river of hot magma flows under the plates. The movement of the magma causes the plates to slowly shift. Sometimes the plates move away from each other. Sometimes they hit against each other. Volcanoes can occur as a result of this underground movement.

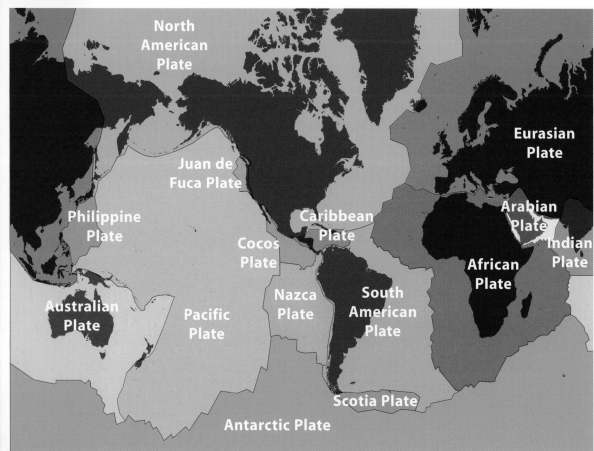

- The Pacific Plate is the largest tectonic plate. It is nearly 9,000 miles (14,484 km) wide.

Locating Volcanoes

Most active volcanoes are found around the Pacific Ocean. The volcanoes form a pattern along the edges of the tectonic plates. As a group, these volcanoes are called the "Ring of Fire."

There are 1,500 active volcanoes above sea level. Not all volcanoes are above sea level. Most of the world's volcanoes are under the sea. Some underwater volcanoes grow over time. Their size increases as new layers of lava harden on top of old layers of lava. Underwater volcanoes can break through the water's surface. They form islands. This is how the Hawai'ian Islands formed.

Earth Erupting

Earth's interior is extremely hot. It is so hot that rock can melt. As rock begins to melt, gas is released. This gas mixes with magma. The gas makes the magma so light that it rises to Earth's surface. The magma collects in a chamber under the volcano.

As more and more magma enters the chamber, pressure builds. The heat of the magma melts or breaks through a weak part of the chamber. The magma eventually bursts through Earth's surface via this passage. Over time, other vents will appear in the mountain.

● The amount of gas in magma affects an eruption. The more gas there is in magma, the more violent the eruption.

Kinds of Eruptions

There are different ways that volcanoes can erupt. Some eruptions are very powerful and scary. Others are weak and less scary.

Explosive eruption: Some eruptions eject liquid and partly solid lava and pieces of rock. These eruptions are called explosive eruptions. Sometimes these eruptions can last several hours. Sometimes they last for days.

Nonexplosive eruption: Nonexplosive eruptions usually occur in Hawai'ian volcanoes. Lava leaks through the sides of a volcano. The lava flows, destroying everything in its path.

Active volcanoes have erupted in the past few hundred years. If a volcano has not erupted for a few hundred years, but has erupted in the last several thousand years, it is called dormant. An extinct volcano is a volcano that has not erupted for several thousand years.

Inside a Volcano

Have you ever imagined looking inside a volcano? This would be very dangerous. Scientists have studied volcanic rocks and Earth's surface. They have even studied volcanoes on other planets. They have discovered that all volcanoes share some common features.

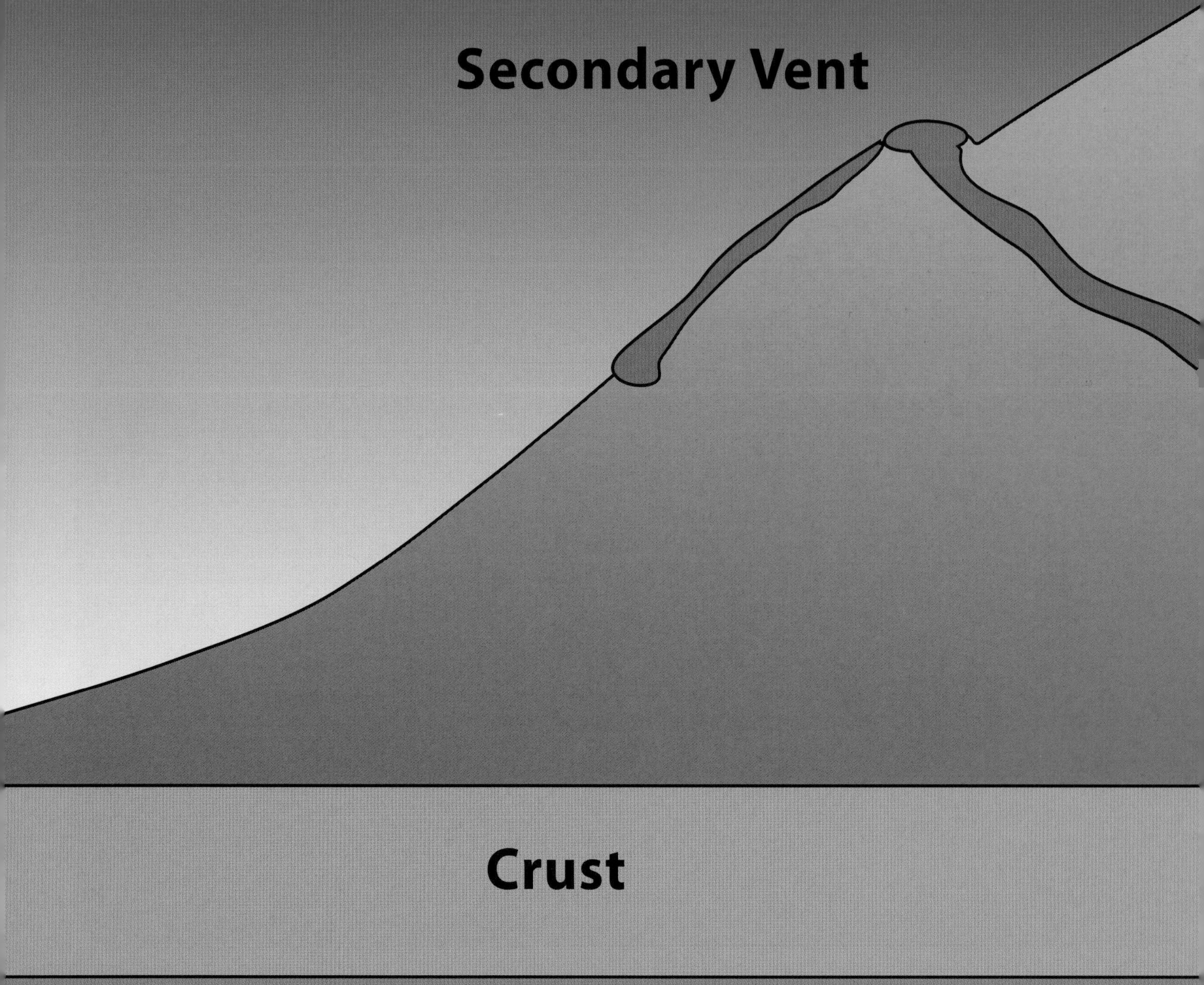

Secondary Vent

Crust

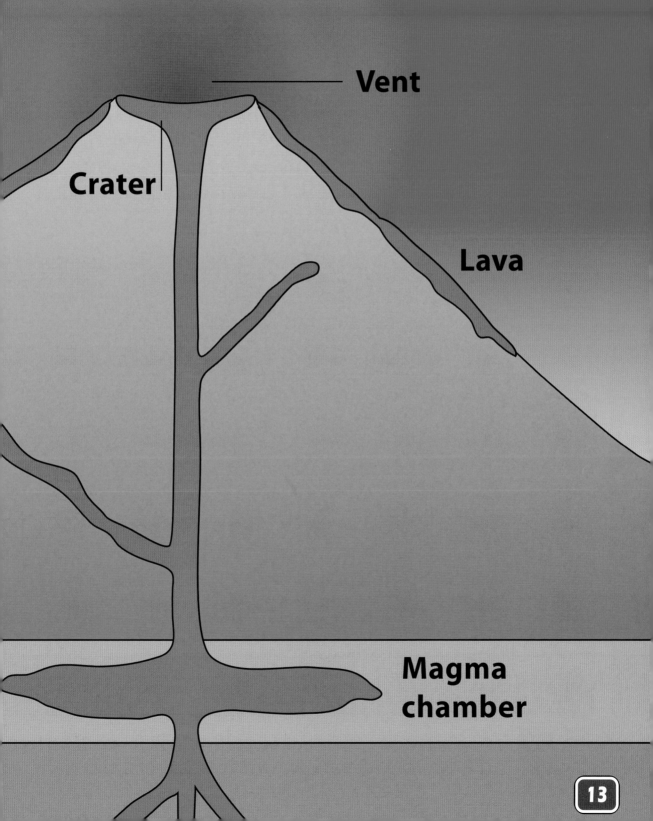

Ash, gas, and cloud

Vent

Crater

Lava

Magma
chamber

Near Volcanoes

Imagine living near a volcano. Maybe you do. Mount St. Helens is located in Washington State. This mountain is near the Pacific Coast. It is part of the Ring of Fire. Mount St. Helens erupted on May 18, 1980. A huge explosion spewed gas and ash 12 miles (19 km) into the air. Fifty-seven people died. Many plants and animals were also killed. A large piece of the mountain tore off.

• Before Mount St. Helens erupted in 1980, it was 9,760 feet (2,975 m) tall. After, it was 8,525 feet (2,598 m) tall.

Volcano Hazards

Would you be afraid to live beside an active volcano? People who live near active volcanoes face many frightening hazards.

Ash and dust

Ash and dust can cover large areas. They can destroy crops and plant life. They can also kill people.

Lava flows

Some types of lava flow very quickly. People do not always have time to leave the area. Hot lava can kill.

Volcanic gases

Gases are released into the atmosphere during an eruption. These gases can be poisonous. People may die if they breathe in the gas.

Mudflows

Mudflows caused by an eruption are known as *lahars*. They are caused when rain mixes with ash. Lahars destroy everything in their path.

Tidal waves

Underwater volcanoes cause tidal waves. These waves are called *tsunamis*. Tsunamis can flood coastal areas and kill people.

Scary Science

Volcanologists study volcanoes. Their work can be dangerous. Sometimes volcanologists study active volcanoes. They have to wear special clothing. **Insulated** suits protect their skin from the heat.

Why would a person choose such a dangerous job? Studying volcanoes is important. Volcanologists can **predict** eruptions. What they learn can save lives.

● It is important for volcanologists to study geology. Geology is the study of Earth's rocks.

Special Rocks

Volcanoes are not always harmful. They can create good soil for farming. They also produce volcanic rock, which can be valuable.

Volcanic rock forms when lava hardens. Volcanic rock is igneous rock. There are different types of igneous rock. This is because there are different kinds of lava. Some of the best-known igneous rocks are basalt, granite, pumice, and obsidian.

Basalt is the most common type of igneous rock. It is used to build roads. Granite is used in construction. People use pumice to scrub away dry skin. Obsidian looks like black glass and is used in jewelry. Sometimes precious stones are found in igneous rock. Such stones include diamonds, rubies, and opals.

Volcano Science

Volcanologists use different methods and equipment to study volcanoes. They track volcanic activity using **observatories** and maps. They study volcanic rock in laboratories.

An important tool used to study volcanoes is a seismometer. This tool measures **tremors** in the ground and helps predict volcanic eruptions. Volcanologists also use **lasers** to record changes in the ground around volcanoes. This gives clues about volcanic activity.

• Seismographs are used to predict volcanic eruptions. A seismograph measures and records Earth's vibrations.

Explosive Myth

Volcanoes are named after Vulcan, the Roman god of fire. Early Romans believed that Vulcan lived beneath Vulcano Island.

Early Romans found a smoking island off the coast of Sicily. They believed the god of fire made lightning deep inside. They named the island Vulcano. The island is still there today.

Surfing Our Earth

How can I find more information about volcanoes?
- Libraries have many interesting books about volcanoes.
- Science centers are great places to learn about volcanoes.
- The Internet offers some great Web sites dedicated to volcanoes.

Where can I find a good reference Web site to learn more about volcanoes?
Encarta Homepage
www.encarta.com
- Type any volcano-related term into the search engine. Some terms to try include "tectonic plates" and "volcano."

How can I find out more about volcanoes and recent eruptions?
U.S. Geological Survey Volcano Hazards Program
http://volcanoes.usgs.gov
- This Web site offers video clips of erupting volcanoes, a volcano glossary, and the latest news on volcanoes around the world.

Science in Action

Make Your Own Volcano
This activity should be done with
an adult.

You will need:
* a foam tray
* a cone-shaped party hat
* an empty film canister
* papier-mâché
* 1 tablespoon (15 mL)
  baking soda
* vinegar, dyed with red food coloring

Directions:
* Place the foam tray on a table covered with newspapers.
* Cut a hole in the top of the party hat. Fit the film canister snugly
  into the hole.
* Set the hat on the tray. Be sure the opening of the film canister
  faces the ceiling.
* Cover the hat and tray with papier-mâché. Do not cover the
  opening of the film canister. Let the volcano dry overnight.
* Put the baking soda into the top of the volcano.
* Poke a few holes in the baking soda with a toothpick. Pour red
  vinegar into the top of the volcano.
* Watch your volcano erupt!

What Have You Learned?

1 What is the name for the group of volcanoes found along the Pacific Ocean?

2 What is magma called when it is outside of a volcano?

3 What is the name of Earth's largest volcano?

4 What kind of volcano is formed by an eruption of basalt lava?

5 What is a scientist who studies volcanoes called?

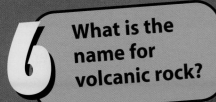

6 What is the name for volcanic rock?

7 There are two types of volcano hazards. True or false?

8 When did Mount St. Helens erupt?

9 What is the name for mudflows caused by an eruption?

10 What tool is used to measure volcanic tremors?

Answers: 1. Ring of Fire **2.** Lava **3.** Mauna Loa **4.** Shield volcano **5.** A volcanologist **6.** Igneous rock **7.** False. There are more than five types of volcano hazards. **8.** May 18, 1980 **9.** Lahars **10.** A seismometer

Words to Know

atmosphere: air, a mixture of gases surrounding Earth

basalt: a type of volcanic rock that is hard, black, and often glassy

erupting: ejecting gas, steam, ash, or lava out of a volcano with great force

insulated: prevented heat from coming through

lasers: devices that make very thin and strong beams of light

lava: hot, melted rock that comes out of an erupting volcano

magma: very hot liquid rock deep inside Earth

observatories: places that have telescopes used for studying the Sun, the Moon, planets, and stars or volcanoes

predict: guess based on special knowledge

tremors: shaking

vent: an opening from which gases or volcanic material escapes

Index